Wolf Coloring Book
An Adult Coloring Book of Zentangle Designs Including Black Background and Mandala Patterns

By Peaceful Mind Adult Coloring Books

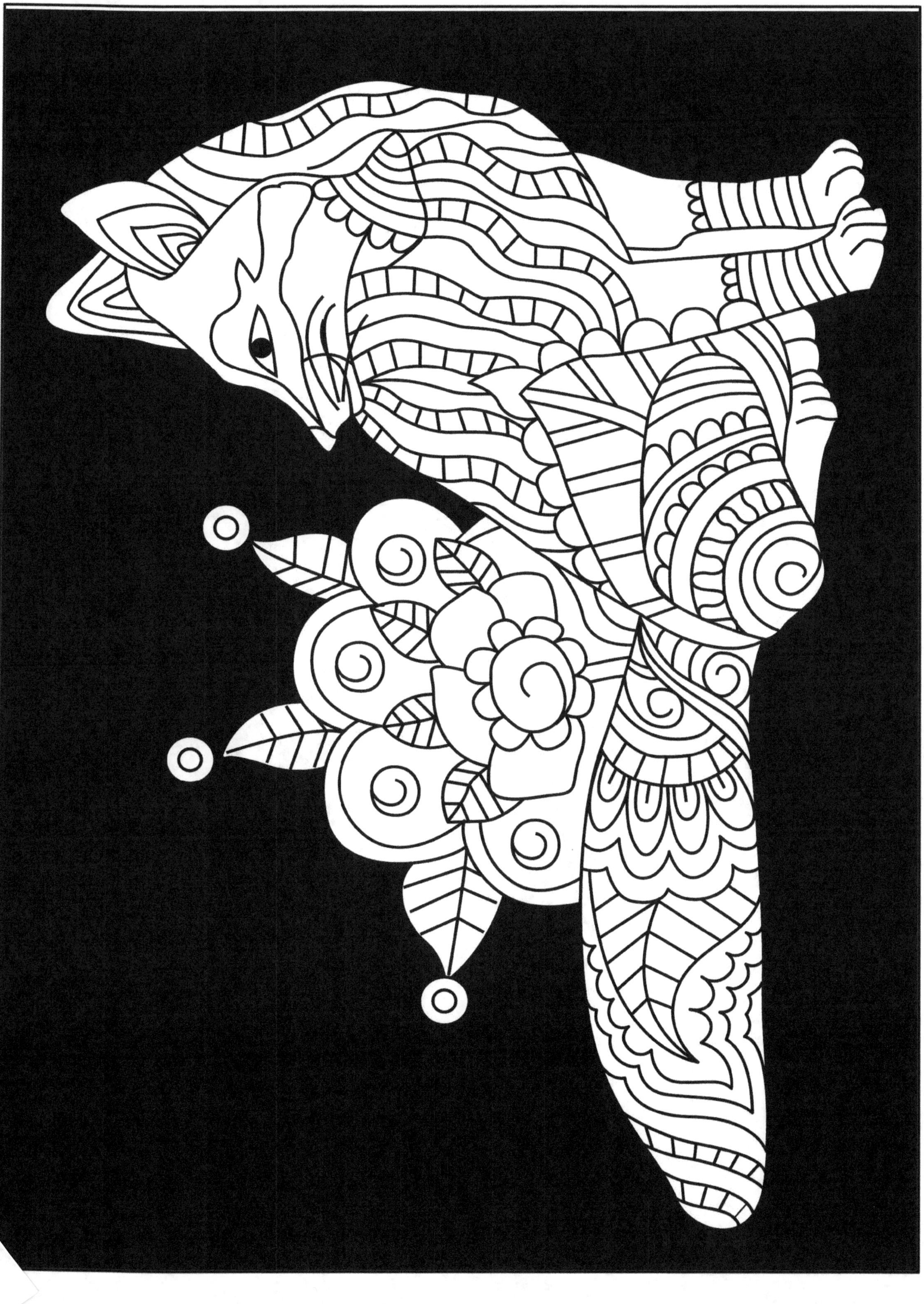

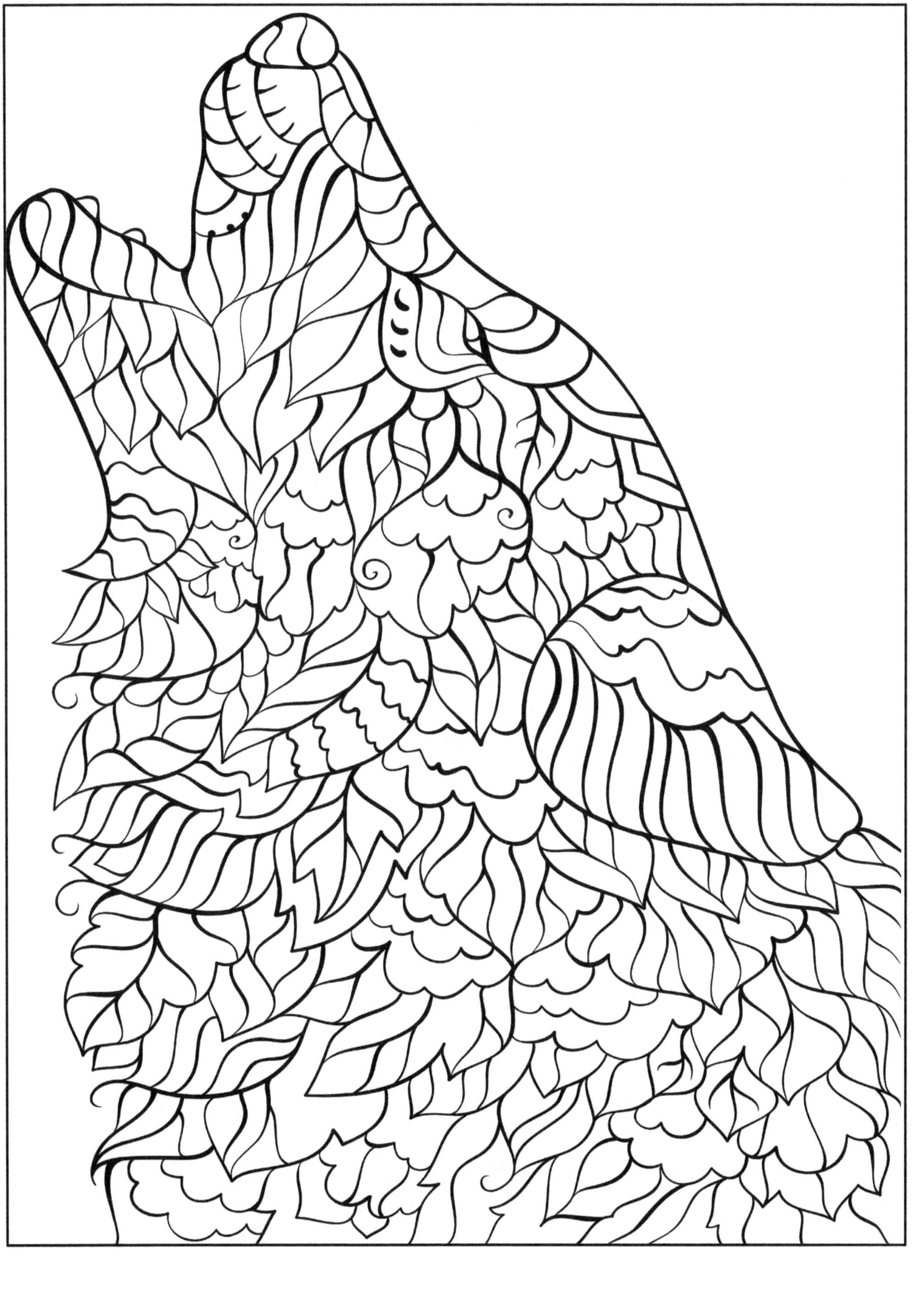

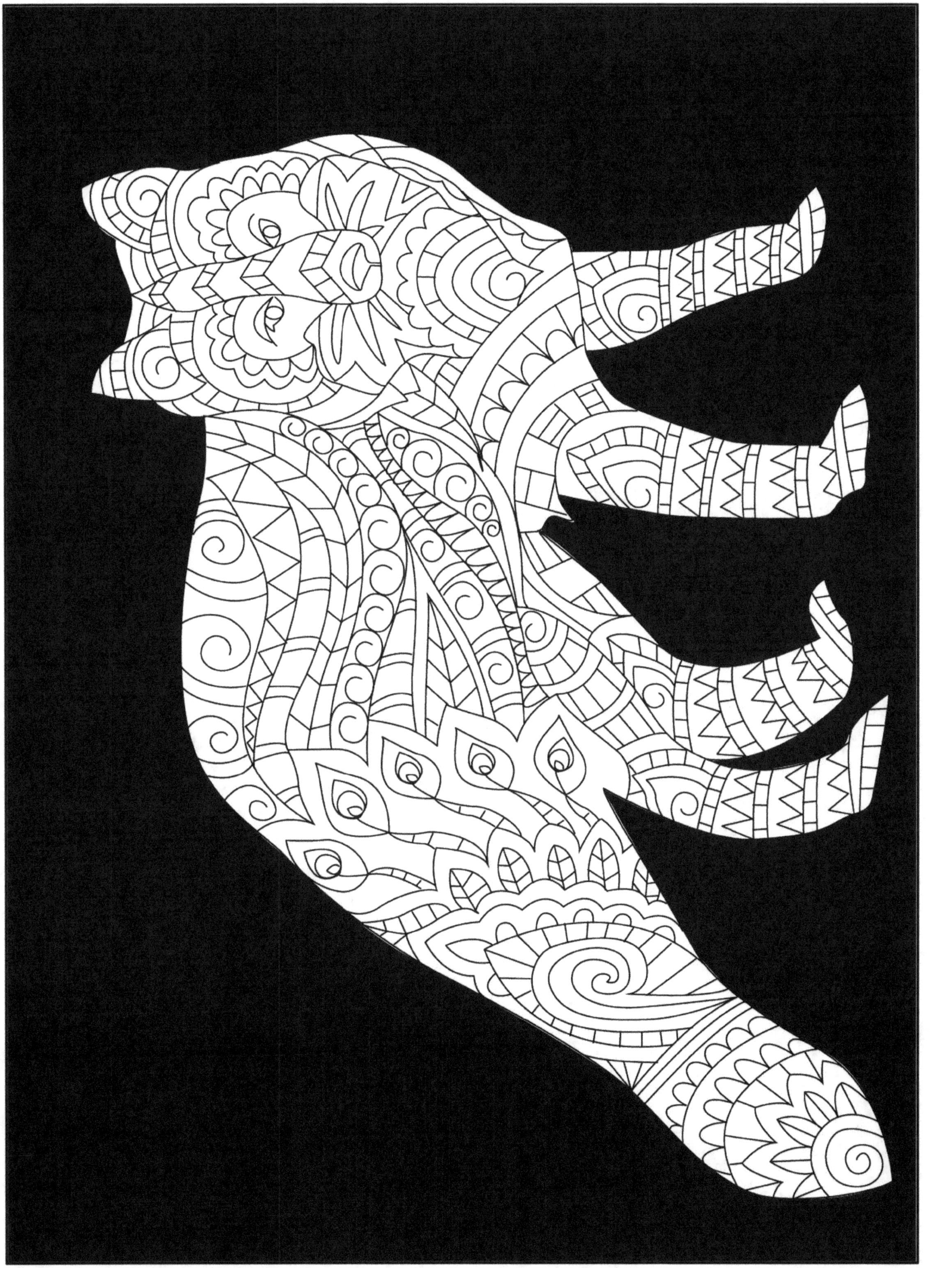

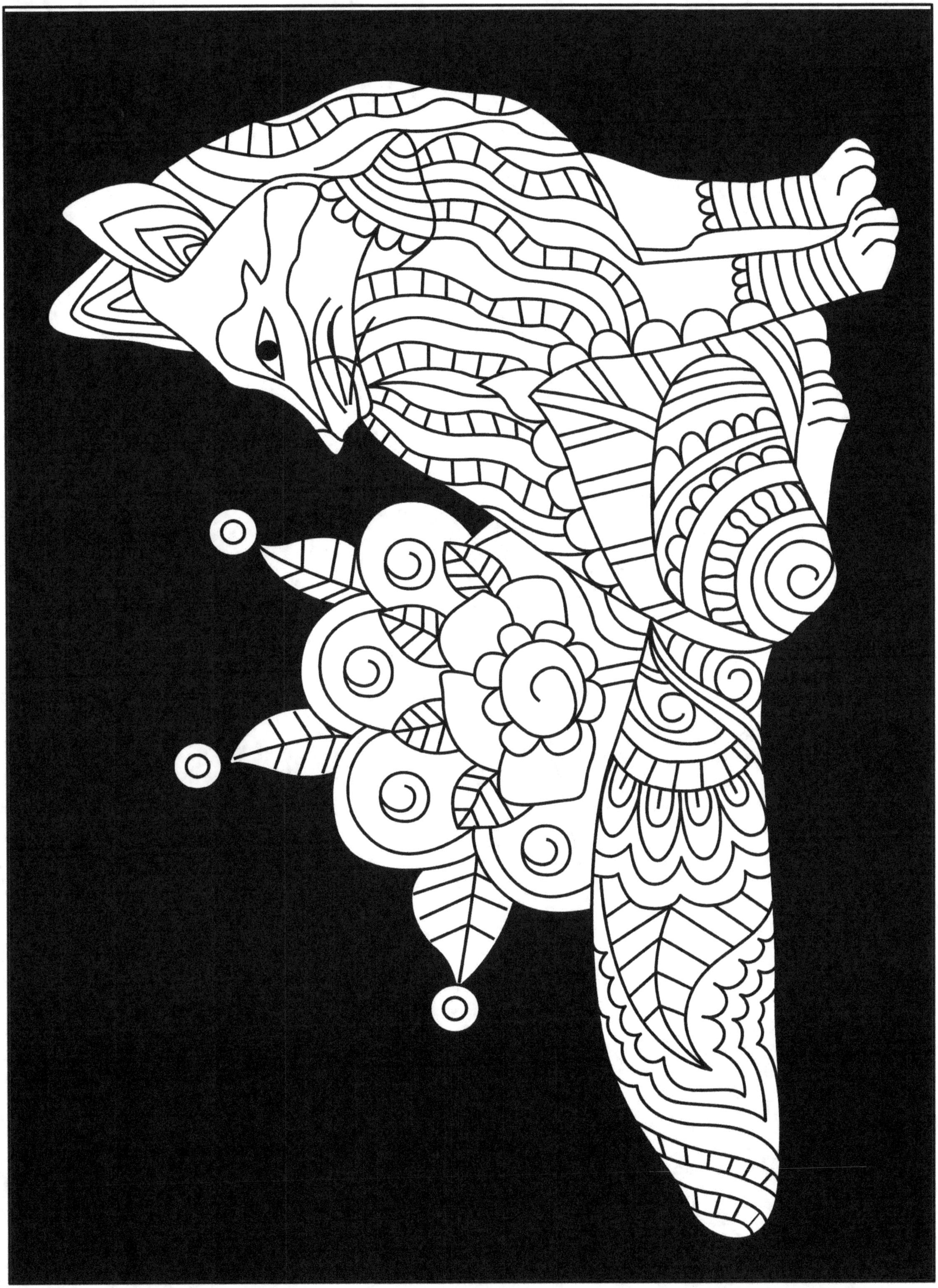

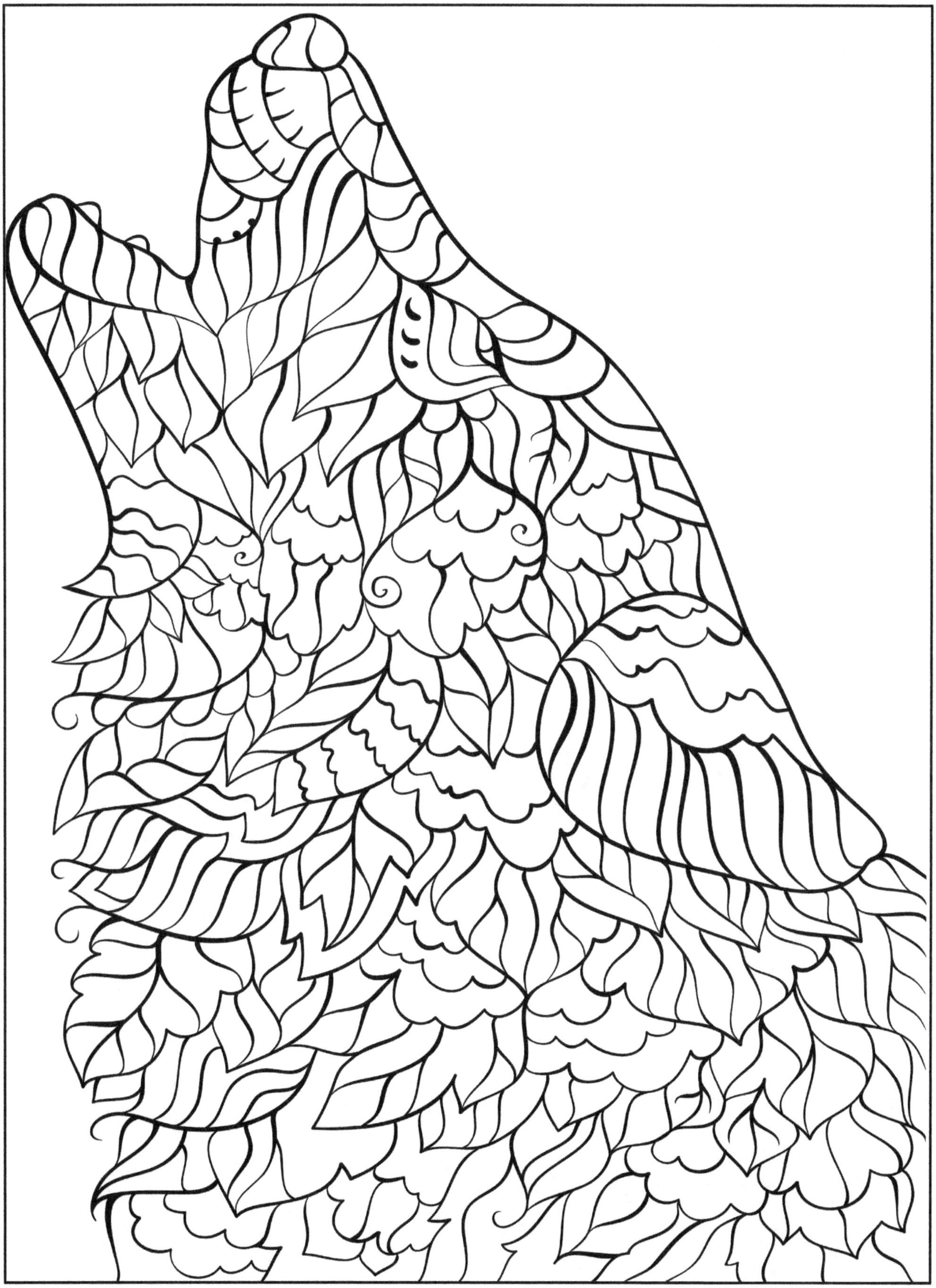

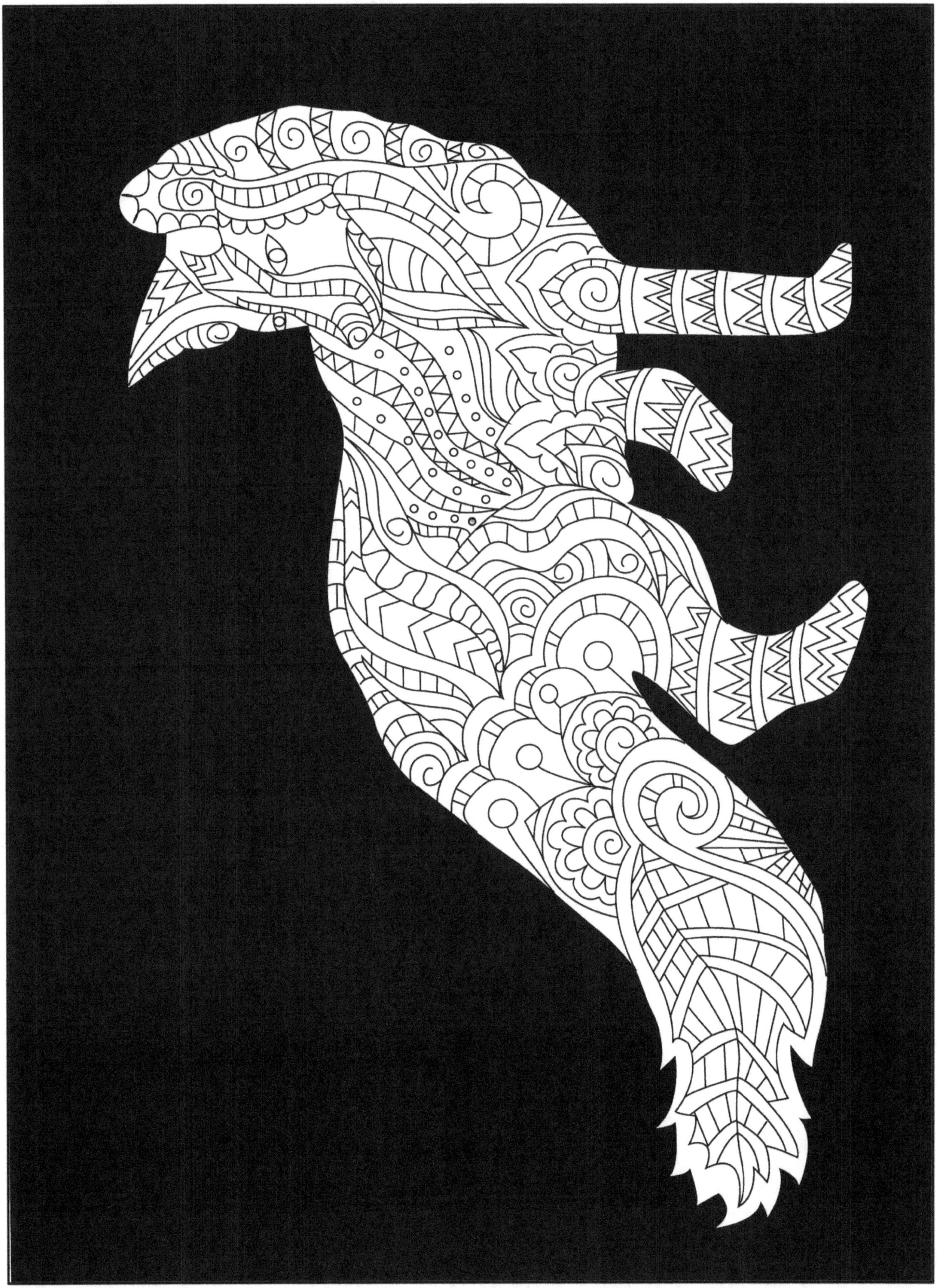

www.ingramcontent.com/pod-product-compliance
Lightning Source LLC
Chambersburg PA
CBHW082013290526
45787CB00017B/3286
* 9 7 8 1 5 4 8 3 1 1 1 8 6 *